Indian Dances

RAM AVTAR 'VIR'

MUSIC PROFESSOR

and

TARA RAMASWAMY

Director, Delhi Institute of Music, Dance & Dramatics

PANKAJ PUBLICATIONS

NEW DELHI

Revised Edition 1998

ISBN 81-87155-02-7

Published by
Pankaj Publications
M-114 Vikas Puri
New Delhi-110018

Sole Distributors :
Cambridge Book Depot
3, Regal Buildings
Sansad Marg,
New Delhi
Phone : 3363395
Fax : 91-11-5141173

Type setting at
Paragon Computers
B-36, Chanakya Place
New Delhi-110059
☎ 5509417

Printed at
Sudershna Printers Delhi - 92

PANKAJ PUBLICATIONS

Preface

The movement of body and steps in proper rhythm and item is essential in all dances in the same way as Swar and Tal exercises are essential in vocal and instrumental music.

Dance is divided into two parts:-

1. Nrita—Nrita means only dance i.e. the movement of bodily organs in proper rhythm and time. It does not display any sort of story or drama etc.

2. Nritya—Nritya means to display the ideas of some drama or story through the movement of bodily organs with dance in proper rhythm and time and in proper uniform. The object of Nritya is to create interest in audience by the motions of the body.

The present book deals with only the exercises on Nritya. This will prove a great help to the beginner without the help of regular teacher. The book depicts the clear picture of movement of organs of body. The pictures themselves are enough to make the dancer begin well versed in performances and exercises. We have given the bols of Tabla and counting numbers in one, two and three with the movement for action in dance.

I am sure that this book will prove very helpful for the beginner as well as to those who have gained the basic knowledge of the subject.

Veeranwali Bhawan
M-24, Kirti Nagar
New Delhi-110 015

Ram Avtar 'Vir'
Sangeet Acharya

INSTRUCTIONS FOR BEGINNERS

1. Vocal music is by mouth, instrumental by hands and dance by the movement of feet and whole body. The practice of dance in proper time cycle and rhythm is very essential.

2. At the time of dance, the mind should be peaceful, body smart and face in smiling position.

3. The movement of every part of the body used in dance should have proper rhythm time sense. The dancer should show a clear pose on the stroke of feet, arms or hands as needed according to the occasion.

4. At every speed, there should be the counting at specific numbers. In the absence of proper arrangement of time spacing, count of numbers, the help can be taken from any of the relative to keep the stroke by a simple piece of wooden rod or dandiya.

5. No part of the body should remain loose at the time of dance.

6. The practice should be made before having food. The stimulating agents are very harmful to a dancer, hence they should observe prohibition.

7. One should have a regular practice of about 2 hours daily. The cold drink after dance is harmful, hence it should be avoided.

8. The dancer should possess the simple and high ideals in his mind.

Contents

Part I

Part II

Part I

1
Dance For Children

The Indian dance started from the very beginning of human life and changed with the change of time. Before the advent of language man used to express the inner feelings through symbols of bodily organs like feet, hands, head and eyes etc. and afterwards these poses converted in words. The first script was the figures.

In Vedic and Ramayana periods the art of dance was popular and many sorts of sound proofs are brought forward to confirm the idea.

Bharat Natya Shastra is the first book on dance to submit the second proofs of this art. This book has been made the base for the further development in this dancing art. After Bharat Natya Shastra the political conditions of the country brought some changes.

The art of music first started in villages then afterwards moving through royal palaces and the holy temples of worship became a means of livelihood. Meanwhile Northern India fell victims of foreign invasions and no proper attention was paid towards the development of this art hence it was seen wandering on the crossroads in search of food and many of the distinguished artists and dancers have to move to south India. In this transitional period the art of dance under perfect control of Rajas, Navabs and the Emperors and the dancer musicians started to show their art to please them. This condition continued upto the end of 19th Century.

In British period too, there was not much appreciable development towards the betterment of this art and majority of artists converted in to professional singers and dancers to earn their living by this art and the general public started to hate instead of appreciating it.

After independence a drastic change is seen in this art. The educated society adopted some inclination towards it . They started to give musical education to their children.

The dance, in spite of being an art of means of amusement, is also a drill to train the children in good discipline and exercise for keeping the body in good health.

The child in the early age possesses weak and elastic bones and muscles. He is unable to take heavy exercises of dance. He requires proper attention to adopt a particular exercise of dance. This book provides very easy and light exercises which can be learnt by him easily and happily.

Bharata has described the poses of feet, hands, arms, waist, breast, head, eyes, and the face of dance. They are very essential for the successful performance but all of them are not needed at a time by particular dance as in very age group a dancer is not expected to display all the organic activities. So it is very essential to have knowledge of age group of the learner. On the basis of above following age groups have been generally accepted :—

1. Child group—up to 6 years.
2. Boy group—from 7 to 12 years.
3. Matured group—from 13 onward.

The child age is an innocent period of human life. It is the period when the child remains under the directions of his parents. The child in this age takes keen interest in copying others. Whatever peculiar things he observes he tries to copy it. The Japanese children are very much interested in such affairs. They are quite perfect to entertain their quest at their houses in the absence of their parents. They try to please them by their songs, stories and dances etc.

Before the invention of modern means of recreation this art was seen among the families but afterwards the recreation by the children has been taken up by the radio, television and theatre etc. In olden times the scope of the family was broader than it is today. People in villages after the whole days hard labour, would assemble on the common platform or the chaupal and passed their leisure time in company of children to enjoy themselves. The child being innocent in very respect needs special attention to be taught by the parents as well as by the teachers.

So in outlining this book I have taken a particular care for the age groups and accordingly distributed the subject matter so that one may not face any sort of difficulty at the time of getting instructions of dance.

The poses have been illustrated by common pictures of dance done by the children of same age group. So no child would feel any difficulty to do them by his own self. Where there is no music and dance teacher this task can easily be taken by the mother of the child through simple reading and understanding the picture.

This book has been written taking all sorts of psychological and age group difficulties in mind and hope it will solve the purpose of the growing children of every age group in best possible way.

EXERCISES

Fig.1: Stand straight join both feet together, keep your wrist at the waist line. The palm may be kept open.

Feet Exercise No. 1

1. Stroke of right toe. 2. Come back in first position.
3. Stroke of left toe. 4. Come back in first position.

Feet Exercise No. 2

Fig.2: Standing position, same as in exercise.
1. Stroke the right foot keeping both feet 30 cm. apart.
2. Come back in first position.
3. Stroke of the left foot keeping both feet 30 cm. apart.
4. Come back in first position. Heel exercise. Standing position same as above.

Heel Exercise

Fig.3: 1. Keeping right foot forward strike the heel.
2. Come back in normal position.
3. Keeping left foot forward strike the heel.
4. Come back in normal position.

Toe Exercise

Fig.4: Standing position same as above.

1. Strike the right toe a bit backward.
2. Come back in normal position.
3. Strike the left toe a bit backward.
4. Come back in normal position.

Arm Exercise No.1

Fig.5:
Standing position same as above.

1. Stretch the right arm rightward.
2. Come in normal position.
3. Stretch the left arm leftward.
4. Come in normal position.

Arm Exercise No.2

Fig.6:
Standing position same as above.

1. Stretch folded hands head ward.
2. Stretch right arm rightward and left arm up with hand in curved pose.
3. Stretch left arm leftward and right arm up with hand in curved pose. Dancing poses in complete dress and make up.

Arm Exercise No. 3

Fig.7:
1. Stretch right arm rightward and bring left arm in front of breast.
2. Bring both arm in front of breast.
3. Stretch left arm leftward and bring right arm in front of breast.

(ii) EXERCISE WITH TATKAR

1st Type

Tatkar may be defined as the bols of dance. They are—ta, thai and tat. Ta stands for foot, thai for toe and heel and tat for double stroke.

The exercises coming onward are to be done by pronouncing bols of dance with tala.

Position of Figures		Right foot Dha	Right toe Ge	Left foot Na	Left toe Ke
Fig. 1	Feet and Toe exercises	ta	thai	ta t	hai
	Toe and Feet exercises	thai	ta	thai	ta
Fig. 2	Feet exercises	ta	thai	ta	thai
	Reverse	thai	ta	thai	ta
Fig. 3	Feet and Heel exercises	ta	thai	ta	thai
	Heel and Feet exercises	thai	ta	thai	ta
Fig. 4	Feet and Toe exercises				
	with curved legs :	ta	thai	ta	thai
	Toe and Feet exercises	thai	ta	thai	ta
Fig. 5	Feet and Toe exercises				
	with movement of arms	ta	thai	ta	thai

Position of Figures		Right foot Dha	Right toe Ge	Left foot Na	Left toe Ke
	Toe and Feet exercises	thai	ta	thai	ta
Fig. 6	Arm and Toe exercises with bending legs as per figs.2 &3 (Feet and Toe)	ta	thai	ta	thai
	Toe and Feet	thai	ta	thai	ta
Fig. 7	Heel and arms exercises as per figs. 2&3 as Feet and Heel	ta	thai	ta	thai
	Heel and Feet	thai	ta	thai	ta

(iii) EXERCISES WITH TATKAR

2nd Type

Tat bols can be performed as follows :—

By giving double stroke in one matra time.
(a) Giving double stroke by one foot.
(b) Giving double stroke by both feet alternatively.
(c) Giving double stroke by toe and foot alternatively.

Position of Figures	Right Foot	Right Toe	Left Foot	Left Toe
	Dha	Ge	Na	Ke
Fig.1: Feet and Toe exercises				
Tat for single foot				
Toe and feet exercises	tat	Thai	tat	thai
Tat for both feet	tat	Thai thai	tat	thai thai
Fig.2 : Feet exercises				
Tat for single foot	tat	Thai	tat	thai
Tat for both feet	tat	Thai thai	tat	thai thai
Fig.3: Feet and Heel exercises				
Tat for single foot	tat	Thai	tat	thai
Tat for both feet	tat	Thai thai	tat	thai thai
Fig.4: Feet and Toe exercises with Curved legs				
Tat for both feet	tat	Thai	tat	thai
Feet and Toe exercises	tat	Thai thai	tat	thai thai
Fig.5: Feet and Toe exercises with movement of arms				
Tat for single foot	tat	Thai	tat	thai
Tat for both feet	tat	Thai thai	tat	thai thai
Fig.6 :Arm and Toe exercises with bending legs as per figs. 2 & 3				
Tat for single foot	tat	Thai	tat	thai

Position of Figures	Right Foot	Right Toe	Left Foot	Left Toe
	Dha	Ge	Na	Ke
Tat for both feet	tat	Thai thai	tat	thai thai
Fig.7:Heel and arm exercises as per Figs. 2 & 3				
Tat for single foot	tat	Thai	tat	thai
Tat for both feet	tat	Thai thai	tat	thai thai

(iv) EXERCISES WITH TATKAR

3rd Type

Tat bols can be performed as follows :—

By giving double stroke in one matra line.

(a) Giving double stroke by one foot.

(b) Giving double stroke by both feet alternatively.

(c) Giving double stroke by toe and foot alternatively.

(d) Tabol with 99 for rest (feet, toe and heel).

Position of Figures	Right Foot	Right Toe	Left Foot	Left Toe
	Dha	Ge	Na	Ke
Fig. 1: Feet and Toe exercises				
Tat for single foot	tat	thai	tat	ta aa
Tat for both feet	tat	thai thai	tat	ta aa
Fig. 2: Feet exercises				
Tat for single foot	tat	thai	tat	thai
Tat for both feet	tat	tat	thai	aa
Fig. 3: Feet and Heel exercises				
Tat for single foot	tat	thai thai	tat	thai thai
Tat for both feet	tat	tat	thai	aa
Fig. 4: Feet and Toe exercises with curved legs				
Tat for single foot	tat	thai thai	tat	thai thai
Tat for both feet	tat	tat	thai	aa
Fig. 5: Feet and Toe exercises with movement of arms				
Tat for single foot	tat	thai	tat	thai
Tat for both feet	tat	tat	thai	aa
Fig. 6: Arm and Toe exercises with bending legs as per figs. 2 & 3				

Position of Figures	Right Foot	Right Toe	Left Foot	Left Toe
	Dha	Ge	Na	Ke
Tat for single foot	tat	thai thai	tat	thai thai
Tat for both feet	tat	tat thai	aa	
Fig. 7: Heel and Arm exercises as per figs. 2 & 3				
Tat for single foot	tat	thai thai	tat	thai thai
Tat for both feet	tat	tat	thai	aa

2
Body and Its Posture

The learners of dance should bear in mind that at the time of their practice, they should concentrate their mind on the position of their body and its posture. The body should have proper weightage and should not lean to one side or the other. The standing position must have firm feet sama-pada — equal base position — the neck and head at the centre, the arms folded and the wrist at the waist line with the fingers turned towards the back.

The learner should not wear anklets or bells. The arms and the portion below the knee should remain as bare as possible.

Feet Exercise — Stand straight. Join both feet together. Keep your wrist at the waist-line. The palm may be kept open. The body is now ready for movement.

Now, observe the time-cycle and allow the rhythm to be captured by your ears and body.

Now step by step follow the rhythm and strike your feet rhythmically. Lift your foot high enough to be in a position to stamp at each syllable of the rhythm. While doing so, no other part of the body should shake. Strike the foot, one after another in the same place in 4 beat cycle.

(1) The movement of feet.
(2) The movement of heel.
(3) The movement of toe.

Now the fabric of foot work can be used in as many condences as you feel like. The arms of the beginner must know the certain specific placements.

(1) It can be held at the chest.
(2) Opened to the sides.
(3) Rotated in circular order.

Now follow the rhythm of the table and make the dance.
Make efforts to practice at a regular time each day.

3
Tal and Lay

Lay —(Speed)—In ordinary sense Lay mean speed or any regular movement to complete a circle in a definite time. It is a natural harmonious flow of vocal and instrumental sound and also a regular succession of accent. According to the observations there are three types of speed in Indian music. All the percussion instruments are used to control and regularise the musical sound.

The Three types of Lay are:

A—Madhya Lay (Medium or normal speed).
B—Drut Lay (Quick or Fast speed).
C—Vilambit lay (slow speed).

Normal Speed—Normal speed is the time required by musicians to complete a round or a circle of a part of song, tune or dance in easy way without exertion. Normal speed is the base of the remaining two speeds i.e. fast and slow speed.

Fast speed—Fast speed means half the time of normal speed i.e. if a musician requires one minute time to complete a part of song, tune or dance, in normal speed, he will require half of the time taken by the normal speed. In other words we can say that the musician can take two rounds of his difinite part of play in the time required in the normal speed.

Slow speed—In slow speed a musician takes double the time to complete the round required by the medium or normal speed. Suppose, if he complete a round of his play in one minute in normal speed, he will take two minutes to complete the same round.

Tal—In Indian music the time element is an essential process. The regular succession of sound Viberation is necessary to make sound musical. Also in vocal, Instrumental music and dancing, intervals are created to make it melodious. These intervals were created by clapping of hands and hence it is called Tal.

Pakhavaj, Mirdang, Dhol, Nakkara, Duff, Khanjari and Tabla etc., are the instruments used for the purpose of Tal. Out of these musical instruments table is most popular.

The late Indian musicians invented many talas of different matras (Strokes) Khand (Bars) and Boles (words) and fixed the points of 'Sam' Talis and Khalis for every Tal.

Matra— (Stroke)—A matra is taken as the shortest time in which a syllable can be properly pronounced. In medium Rhythm the time of a matra, is presumed to be one second, in fast Rhythm half second and in slow Rhythm two seconds.

Boles—Sound produced by Tabla Dhama or Duggi by the stroke of fingers and hand in different ways is called boles i.e. Ta, Na, Tee, Tin, Ke, Ge, Te, Tay, Dha, Dhe, Dhin.

Theka—The round of a Tal has fixed matras and on every matra there are fixed boles. They are called Thekas.

Tali—Clapping of hands is called Tali i.e. Theka of Talas having Tali points marked 1 2 3 4 etc.

Khali—Khali means a gap of some matras which boles of Theka play by right hand on Tabla only. The left (Duggi or Dhama) remains silent in Khali matra's time.

Khali points help the classical musicians to understand the starting point of their Tala (Sam point) when they sing Khyal, for Khali point on Theka `0' sign on the matra point is shown in every Tal.

Sam—The starting point of Tal is called sam. Say first matra of talas is sam point and on every theka it is shown by + sign.

Note—In this book only Teen Tal Thekas are used.

(i) BOLES OF THEKA TAL KEHARWA (Type 2)

Sam		Khali	
+		0	
1	2	3	4
Chage	Nage	Take	Dhin

(ii) BOLES OF THEKA TAL DHUMALI

Sam				Khali			
+				0			
1	2	3	4	5	6	7	8
Dha	Dhin	Na	Tin	Trak	Dhin	Dhage	Trak

(iii) BOLES OF THEKA TAL KAWALI

Sam				Khali			
+				0			
1	2	3	4	5	6	7	8
Dhin	Dhin	Dha	Dha	Tin	Tin	Tha	Tha

4
Exercise According to Pictures

Namaskar

Namaskar bringing folded hands in front of breast, stand in prayer position bowing head slightly downward.

Namaskar is performed by 3 girls in normal position in straight line.

(i) STANDING POSITION

Stand straight joining both feet together, keeping wrist at the waist line. Palm may be kept open.

Taking right turn stretch both hands up prayer pose strike left to backward.

Fig. 11:

Bring right hand in front of breast and the left up making lotus shape by both hands.

Fig. 12:

The body should remain twisted leftward balancing the body on right leg and the left keeping up at right angle. Bring both heads in front of breast with hands one upon the other. Sighting forward or rightward.

Fig. 13:

Balancing the body on left leg bring folded hand over head and the right leg behind the left leg.

Fig. 14 :

Keeping both hands folded over head stand in normal position.

Fig. 15:

Bending both arms at about 45° bring hands in finger pose.

Fig. 16:

Lefting right foot up rest it on left leg and keeping knee curved bend the right hand inward and left downward body being balanced on left leg.

Fig. 17:

Keeping left foot forward strike with right toe and the left hand may be stretched forward.

Fig. 18:

Come in position shown as fig. 16 (two girls).

Fig. 19:

Swing both hand downward and start dancing with stroke of right heel and half toe.

Figs. 20 & 21:

Strike the right heel. Keeping right foot forward and dance by the blt. toe. Stretch right arm out and bring left in front of breast pose in hand and finger pose. Dancing 2 girls in full swing.

Fig. 22:

In dancing position bring both hands over head holding one on another by fingers.

Fig. 23:

Two girls dancing, stretching both hands outward in a position that they may hold one another by hands as shown.

Fig. 24:

Three girls dancing in group two holding hands together and the third putting her right hand on the left shoulder of central girl.

Fig. 25:

Three girls dancing in different poses and first girl with hands in front of face second in front breast and the third over head.

(ii) KRISHNA AND SAKHIS DANCE

Fig. 26:

Lord Krishna playing on flute.

Fig. 27:

Three girls dancing bring left hand over breast and the right stretching outward.

Fig. 28:

Dance in sitting position keeping hands curved.

Fig. 29:

Dance in sitting position keeping left hand out and right bending sideward.

Fig. 30:

Two girls dancing in sitting poses bring their right hands on heads and left stretching out with palms downward.

Fig. 31:

Three girls dancing in sitting position stretching both hands outwards.

(iii) SITTING POSITION

Fig. 28:

Half sitting on both feet in hand poses.

Fig. 29:

Half setting on one knee in hand and arm poses.

(iv) DANCE ON NAMASKAR POSTURES

Fig. 32:

1. Namaskar in folded hands in front of breast.
2. Namaskar in beginning posture stretching both hands up.
3. Namaskar with right hand in front of breast and the left stretching out above the shoulders.

Fig. 33:

Poses of different types of dances.

Fig. 34:

Poses of different types of dances.

Fig. 35:

Poses of different types of dances.

Standing Position

Back Step

Hands Position

Hands over Head

Standing on one Foot

Arm Position

Krishna And Sakhis

5
Dance on Namaskar Postures

You have made practice of dance with the help of figs. 1 to 31 of different postures. Now you will be made conversant with the definitions of two words—Tatkar and Thata.

Tatkar: Tatkar may be defined as the bols of dance. They are three—ta, thai and tat. All the remaining bols are made with the combination of these three. Now you are advised to make practice on the basis of counting only.

Thata: That means stage opening postures and actions i.e. the manners of standing on the stage at the time of opening of the stage and the dance should be started in the same actions.

First of all we are giving you the actions of dance in the postures of Namaskar. Have practice according to them.

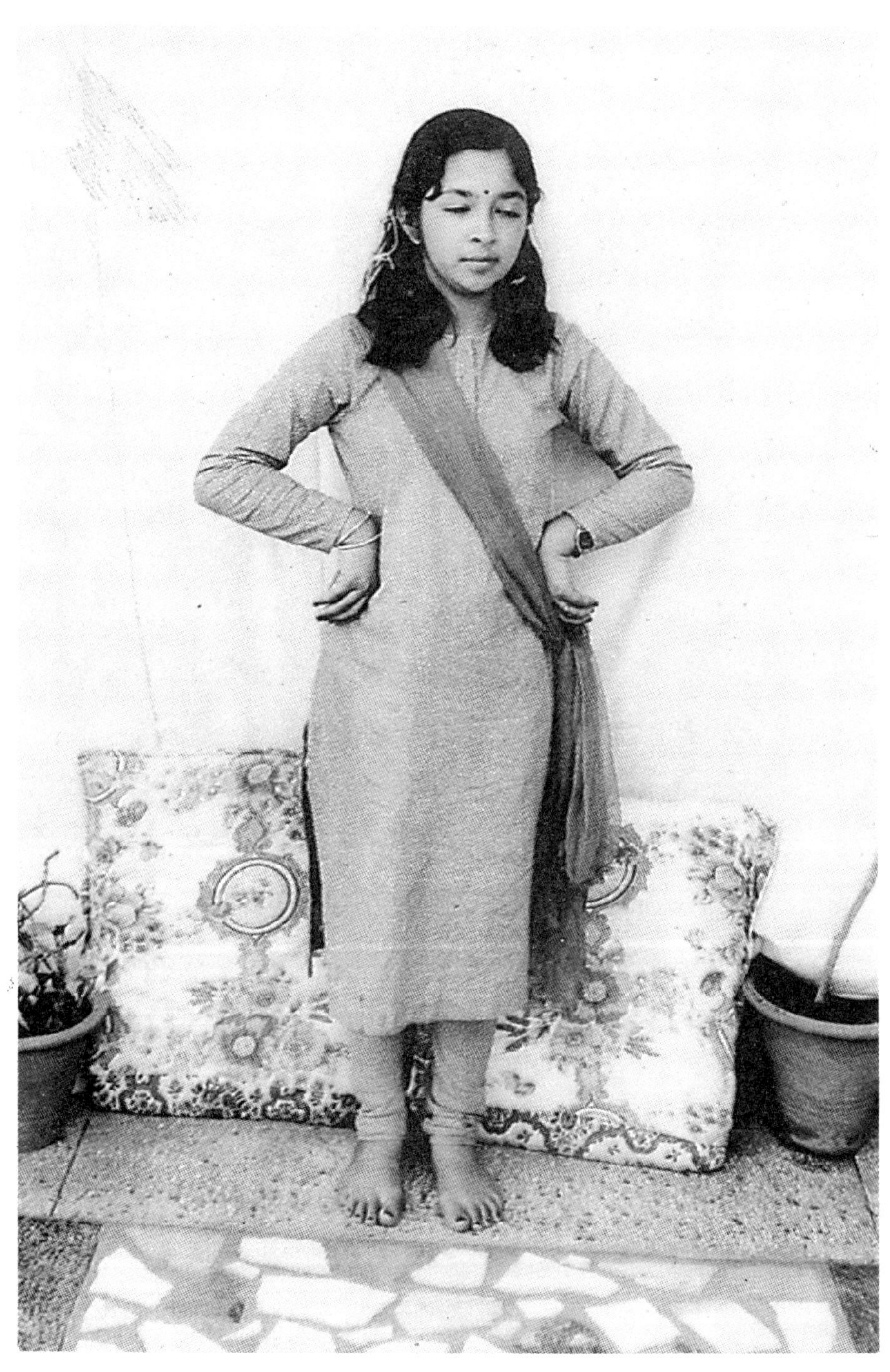

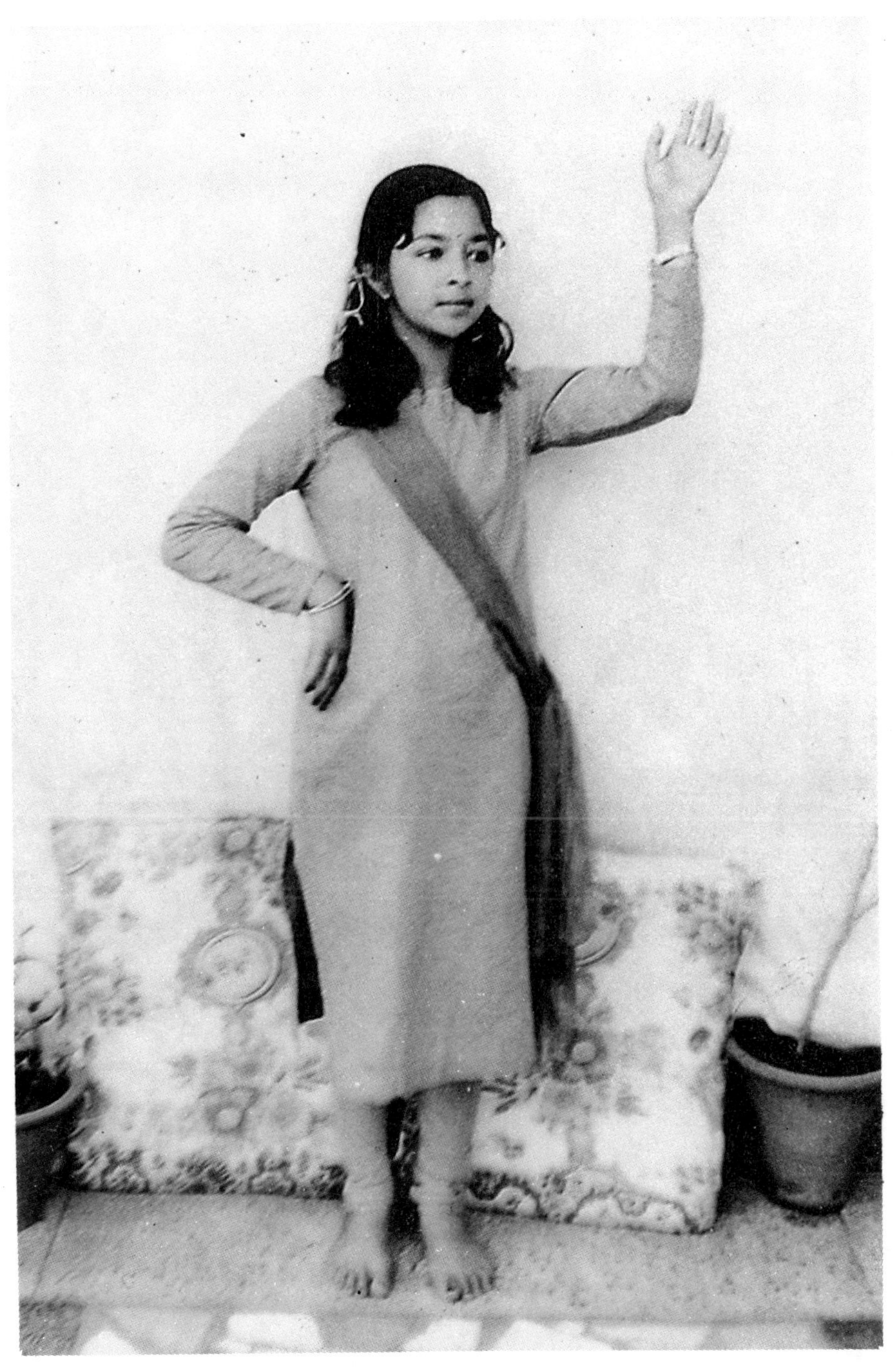

Part II

6
Preliminary Steps and Postures of Body

Dancing is an art. It is associated with human life and is closely related to culture and civilization of a country and its people. It is as old as the man himself for it is one of several well-known means for entertainment for the rich and the poor alike.

Dancing, as an art, has been popular in India since times immemorial. It was popular in Vedic Period. It was performed during the Buddha Period. Hindu and Muslim rulers, princes and noble men patronized dancers (and singers) during the Mughal Period. The art was practised in temples also. That lent colour to the worship of Gods.

It did, however, suffer during the medieval period when the Turks, Afghans and others invaded India again and again. That resulted in political instability in Northern India and forced learned men, and artists to seek refuge in Southern India. They were received there with open arms by the rulers and ruled there. They too made useful contribution to the enrichment of the cultural life of the people through this fine art.

It also waved during the British Period when it became the profession of morally low people. It was, however, susticated after India regained independence. Since then, the successive Governments at the Centre and in the States provided all sorts of encouragement and patronage with the result that several versatile dancers have been enriching the cultural life of the people. That has attracted the attention of the younger generation. The subject is now being taught in Public Schools and other Educational Institutions. But because of dearth of suitable books on the subject, students and other enthusiasts have been feeling handicapped in learning the art. This guide was, therefore, originally published in 1979 to fill that gap. Since it evoked appreciative response from the students in general and their teachers in particular, a second edition was brought out the same year.

On the persistent demand of students and others, this revised and enlarged edition has been brought out. Every effort has been made to make it more useful and educative for the students and others who would like to learn the art at home without the aid of teachers and instructors.

Special care has been taken to use simple language and to illustrate various steps and poses in a lucid manner. It is hoped that it would serve the purpose for which it has been brought out.

(i) TYPES OF DANCE

Indian classical dances are of the following types:—

a. Kathak
b. Kathakali
c. Bharat Natyam
d. Manipuri
e. Orissi, and
f. Light Classical Dances.

Kathak, Kathakali, Bharat Natyam, Manipuri and Orissi dances are complicated ones. They have special techniques. It takes time to learn them. They cannot be learnt at home, without the guidance of a tutor. This book, therefore, does not cover such dances. It covers light classical dances only which an enthusiastic child will be able to learn and practise at home with or without the help of a tutor. Various pictures included in this book clearly depict the movements of various organs and a careful, child should be able to understand and immitate them without any difficulty. It also contains the boles of Tabla with reference to counting of numbers as one, two and three to keep time and rhythm in the movement of feet and other organs in dance.

I am sure this book will serve its purpose and benefit not only the beginners but also those who are familiar with the initial steps but are not yet perfect in the art. For those who have already learnt the art but not yet mastered it, another book entitled *Natraj–Indian Dances through the Ages*–was published in 1982. That was appreciated by one and all not only in India but also in other countries as well. That covers dances popular during the Buddha Period, Muslim Period, Classical Dances as well as international dances. That also contains many illustrations with playing on Tabla which indicate the tune, tal, time and rhythm as also poses suitable for various dances.

(ii) GENERAL INSTRUCTIONS FOR BEGINNERS

1. Music is of two kinds :— Vocal and Instrumental.

A sweet sound produced by mouth is called Vocal music. The one produced by an instrument is termed Instrumental Music. Dance is performed on the basis of both vocal and instrumental music. The word Sangeet in Sanskrit includes vocal, instrumental music and dance.

2. Dancing should be practised bearing in mind the importance of time and rhythm.

3. At the time of dancing, the dancer must maintain mental equilibrium and poise. His/Her mind should be peaceful and alert. His/Her body should be smart. He/She should have a smiling face indicating a cheerful mood.

4. Every limb and part of the body used in a dance should move rhythmically and timely. The dancer should present a clear pose simultaneously with the stroke of feet, arms or hands as the occasion demands.

5. At every speed, specific numbers 1, 2, 3, etc. should be counted to ensure spacing of time. In the absence of proper arrangements for counting of numbers and time spacing, any friend or relative may be asked to help by keeping time with the help of a simple wooden rod or a stick called **daisdiya**.

6. Every limb of the dancer should look smart and tight. None should be loose at the time of dancing.

7. Dancing should be practised before eating food.

8. Intoxicating and stimulating agents are very harmful. They should be avoided.

9. Practice makes a dancer perfect. A regular practice for two hours a day is recommended.

10. Cold drinks after practice or performance are harmful and should be dispensed with.

11. Dancers should be motivated. They should be imbued with high ideals, morals and exemplary character.

(iii) GENERAL DIRECTIONS FOR DANCERS IN THE AGE GROUP ABOVE 13

You would have practised dances outlined in the fore-going pictures. But it is very essential to observe the following directions while performing dances :—

1. Before appearing on the stage, make-up, dress, robe and payals etc. should be thoroughly attended to.

2. At the time of appearing in the stage, the dancer should keep in mind the nature of dance to be performed.

3. The dancer should not look straight into the eyes of the audience. He/She should turn his/her eyes right and left or keep on casting glances on his/her own limbs.

4. When on the stage, hands, feet, head, arms or any other part of the body should not move without rhythm.

5. A smile or sadness on the face or movement of eyes should be in accordance with the story on which the dance is based.

6. A dancer on the stage must not feel shy on any account.

7. The dancer must be self-reliant. He/She should never think that his/her dance is not being appreciated by the audience. On the other hand, he/she should believe firmly that his/her dance is the best.

8. If V.I.P.'s included in the audience, dancers should not hesitate nor should they consider themselves as low. Such ideas can adversely effect the performance.

9. If the audience includes relations or friend of the dancers, the artistes should not exchange glances with them. They should neither smile at them nor should they divert their attention from the dance.

10. The dancer, while dancing should consider himself/herself as a good artiste, concentrate on dancing performing nimbleness and maintaining perfect rhythm.

(iv) DANCE IN SITTING POSITION

It is of two types. The first type consists of making poses of dance in a sitting position, then to stand up dancing in a straight position.

In the second type, the dancer dances, then sits down, continues her dance, and stand up.

The second type of dance is shown in figs. 36 to 48 on pp. 45 to 56 and is being described below:

Fig. 36 Standing up with both the arms spread out and to bend the two hands downward.

Fig. 37 To stand up keeping both the arms on the waist.

Fig. 38 To keep the left hand on the head and stretching the left foot forward, being on the right side and to hang the right arm downward.

Fig. 39 To keep the left hand on the head, stretching the right hand forward and to sit down on the knees.

Fig. 40 Keeping the left hand on the head, stretching the right hand forward, bending the right knee and stretching the left leg.

Fig. 41 Sitting on the two knees with both the hands stretched out.

Fig 42 Right foot forward, both the hands spread as if begging, the upper portion of the body slightly bent forward.

(v) DANCE IN TURNING POSITION

The dancer dances and turns right or left according to her own choice.
She stands up erect with both the hands folded and kept

on the head. (see fig. 36 on p. 45)

Fig. 43 Keeps the right hand raised, the left hand on the waist and strikes her feet against the ground.

Fig. 44 Keeps the left hand raised and the right hand on the waist and strikes her feet against the ground.

Fig. 45 Keeps the left hand raised and right hand on the waist, right foot fixed on the ground, turning the left foot to the right while dancing.

Fig. 46 Remains in the same pose as in (fig. 45) and exposing her back.

Fig. 47 Remaining in the pose as in (fig. 46) and turning to the left.

Fig. 48 Finally, coming back to the original position with left hand raised and right hand on the waist.

What is Dance ?

Dance means movement of body and its various organs with rhythmical steps, glides, revolutions, gestures, etc. It may be performed alone or with a partner or partners and is usually accompanied by vocal instrumental music.

Classical dances provide physical, mental and psychological entertainment. They also provide physical exercise and help its devotees in keeping good health. They feel alert, physically and mentally, after dancing for some time.

(vi) CLASSIFICATION OF DANCE

Dance is classified into **Nrita** and **Nritya**. The former (**Nrita**) means movement of organs in time and rhythm. It does not involve dramatic performance nor does it depict any episode or story. It is mere dance—pure and simple.

The latter (**Nritya**) means not only movement of feet and other organs in time and rhythm but also includes narration of a tale or episode in proper role and through gestures. It also includes expression of human moods and sentiments. The object of **Nritya** is to entertain the audience and to create and sustain their interest in its performance.

(vii) INSTRUCTIONS FOR SELF-LEARNERS

You have learnt dance with the help of pictures, and you have got sufficient matter for dressing up. Now try to perform the folk dances of your country. The choice of proper uniforms should also be done on the same outlines. We have given some examples with pictures such as man reaping crops, group dance with wooden sticks, school group dances and also the dances played by sister and brother etc., try to do them with the help of description also the dances played by sister and brother etc., try to do them with the help of description given with them. The poses of various parts of the body should be the same as described.

The time and rhythm in folk dances varies time to time. You should be very particular about it. The time and the strokes should particularly be noted. The folk dances need smartness and activeness. It should be followed properly. Without these things the dances does not show good results.

In group songs and dances one should be very particular about the actions and the movements of companion.

The dancer should start his performance taking himself as the actual man whom he is going to represent through his dance.

In Hori etc., the use of syiringe should be in proper time and the rhythm and the steps should also be in proper way.

(viii) RAS DANCE

Let the children stand in circle. One of the children playing flute should stand in the middle. All the remaining children should watch over the activities of the middle child. Each one of the children should have a coloured wooden stick of about 60 cm., in hands.

Activity : 1. Let the toe be put together on the ground and stick be struck together at a time. Produce striking sound and then strike the stick against the right hand stick of the child of left hand side. Then striking the toe of the left foot on ground and striking your own stick together again strike right hand stick with the right hand stick of the child of your right side.

2. Again throwing the toe of right foot on ground strike both the sticks together and also strike both of your sticks against the stick of the child to your left in such a way that your left and right hand sticks should strike against the right and left hand sticks respectively. Then repeat the same by throwing left foot on ground. Striking your left and right hand sticks against the right and left hand sticks of the child to your right side.

3. Then put the toe of your right foot on ground and strike your sticks together and then strike your right hand stick against the stick of right hand child and the left hand stick against the right hand stick of your left hand child.

Go on moving in circle repeating all the three activities and developing the speed gradually and stop the dance in Drut laya or fast rhythm.

(ix) DANCE OF SISTER AND BROTHER

This dance is performed by two girls one sister and the other brother.

1. Both the children should strike the right foot on ground and then putting right hand on waist raise the other hand to form a flower like pose with fingers.

2. Putting the punja of right foot on the ground raise the left hand up and make the flowery figure with fingers.

3. Strike the toe of right foot on gound bring right hand against breast and then stretch the left hand out.

4. Strike the toe of left foot on ground and bring the left hand against the breast and then stretch right hand out.

5. The boy should strike the right foot in pose of playing flute and the girl dancing in fast rhythm should keep aside.

6. Then the girl dancing in fast rhythm should come to the boy.

7. Girl should keep on moving and dancing in pose of pitcher on head and the boy dancing in fast rhythm should move forward.

8. Then the boy should come near the girl in dancing pose.

(x) SONG WITH DANCE

This dance is performed with song. There should be four groups possessing two or more children in each. The movement of feet is as described before.

The first part of the song is to be sung by the whole group and the Second, Third, Fourth and Fifth parts by the different groups separately and in the end all should return to their original place singing the first part of the song.

First part to be sung with dance

Song with dance	:	Nacho ! nacho ! nacho ! nacho ! Gao khushee ke geet.
Only dance	:	Chhun chhun chhun Chhun chhun chhun.
Song and dance	:	Payal kee dhun men Bhare hue hen Lakhon hee gun.
Only dance	:	Chhun chhun chhun Chhun chhun chhun.

Second part for first group (steping forward)

Song and dance : Gao milkar nacho bhaiya
gao khushee ke geet
Jo gaye muskaye jagat men
hogee uskee jeet.

Only dance : Chhun chhun chhun
Chhun chhun chhun.

Group song with dance : Nacho ! nacho ! nacho ! nacho!
Gao khushee ke geet.

Only dance : Chhun chhun chhun
Chhun chhun chhun.

Third part for the second group (steping forward)

Song with dance : Sare jag ke kan kan men hen
bhaye huye sab rag
Sukh ko apna sabhee samaho
dukh ko do sab tiyag
dukh ko do sab tiyag

Only dance : Chhun chhun chhun
Chhun chhun chhun.

Group song with dance : Nacho ! nacho ! nacho ! nacho !
Gao khushee ke geet.

Only dance : Chhun chhun chhun
Chhun chhun chhun.

Fourth part for the third group (steping forward)

Song with dance : Dekho aae ghir ghir ghir badal
Sare jag par chhaye hen
Tap tap tap barse pany

: Sab ke man ko bhaye hen

Only dance : Chhun chhun chhun
Chhun chhun chhun.

Group song with dance	:	Nacho ! nacho ! nacho ! nacho ! Gao khushee ke geet.
Only dance	:	Chhun ! chhun ! chhun ! Chhun ! chhun ! chhun.

Fifth part for the fourth group (steping forward)

Song and dance	:	Nabh men peeng badhayen Panchhee bankar uden gagan men
	:	Koyal bankar gaen ham
Only dance	:	Chhun chhun chhun Chhun chhun chhun.
Group song with dance	:	Nacho ! nacho ! nacho ! nacho ! Gao khushee ke geet.
Only dance	:	Chhun chhun chhun Chhun chhun chhun.

(xi) GROUP DANCE

Let the children be divided in two groups and stand in two rows facing one another at about 150 cm apart. In dancing actions come closer together first and then again should depart to the original place in same manner and do as follows :—

1. Putting the right foot on gound clap your hands.
2. Putting the left foot on ground take right turn and swing your hands forcefully.
3. Putting your right foot on ground take left turn and swing your hands forcefully.
4. Putting left foot on ground bend forward and clap your hands.
5. Putting your right foot on ground clap your hands.

6. Putting left foot on ground take right turn and swing your hands.
7. Putting the right foot on ground take left turn and swing your hands forcefully.
8. Putting left foot on ground strike your hands with the hands of child in front of your.
9. Then continuing your dance move to your original place.

(xii) NAMASKAR DANCE

This dance is performed by three girls. The girl in centre should be a bit taller than the other two. They should stand in folded hands.

1. Taking right foot a bit forward strike the ground with heel.
2. Then keeping left foot ahead strike the ground with heel.
3. Taking the right foot forward strike ahead and strike the other foot on your own place.
4. Taking left foot ahead strike heel forward and give the other stroke on your place.
5. The girl in the middle raising her hands up should strike the toe of right foot on the ground and the girls to the right and left should hold the waist with one hand and keeping the other hand up should strike the ground with right foot.
6. The girl in the middle should move forward in dancing and the girls to the left and right should take round in dance at their own positions with hands up.
7. The girl in the middle then should move ahead dancing with folded hands and the girls on sides should go on dancing and then sit on knees on half standing positions.

(xiii) PRAYER SONG

Mere Prabhoo mujhko bata
Tere siva men kiya karoon?

Teree saran ko chhodkar,
Jag kee saran ko kiya karoon?

Phoolon men bas rahe ho tum,
Kaliyon men khil rahe ho tum,

Mere to man men too hee hai
Mandir men jake kiya karoon

Chanderma ban kar aap hee
Taron men jag maga rahe

Teree chamak ke samane
Deepak jala ke kiya karoon.

(xiv) GROUP SONG

1. Kadam kadam barayae ja
Khushi ke geet gaae ja
Yeh zindgi hai desh ki
Too desh pe lootae ja

2. Veeron ke santaan hai
Unchi teri shaan hai
Veerta se desh ki
Shaan ko barahae ja
Desh ko jagae ja

3. Zindgi teri amar
Marane se hargiz na dar
Veer var too aageh barh
Shatruon pe chhae ja
Veerta dikhae ja

4. Bhed bhav door kar
Ekta ke bhav par
Phir banega desh amar
Sab ko ek banae ja
Sab ko rah dikhae ja